THE BATTLEFIELD PHOTOGRAPHER

ALSO BY CARMINE SARRACINO

POETRY

The Idea of the Ordinary (an Orchises Book)

The Heart of War

NON-FICTION

The Porning of America

THE BATTLEFIELD PHOTOGRAPHER

CARMINE SARRACINO

Life is fired at us point blank.
—JOSÉ ORTEGA Y GASSET

WASHINGTON
ORCHISES
2008

Library of Congress Cataloging-in-Publication Data

Sarracino, Carmine, 1944-
   The battlefield photographer / Carmine Sarracino.
      p. cm.
   ISBN 978-1-932535-16-7 (alk. paper)
      1. United States—History—Civil War, 1861-1865—Poetry.
   I. Title.
   PS3619.A75B38 2008
   811'.6—dc22
                                    2007022515

ACKNOWLEDGEMENTS

Beloit Poetry Journal: "The Courage of Sergeant Miller," "The Cowardice of Corporal Hughes"; *The Bryant Literary Review:* "Hospital Ships"; *Contemporary Poets on Pennsylvania:* :"Armory Square Hospital," "The Battlefield Museum Guide Speaks"; *Encore:* "Letter from Shiloh"; *The Laurel Review:* "Mary Chesnut at Mulbery House; *Prairie Schooner:* "Armory Square Hospital, Reconstruction," "The Hero of Gettysburg"; *War in Literature and the Arts:* Sunrise at Gettysburg," "The Battlefield Museum Guide Speaks." A selection of these poems was published as a chapbook, *The Heart of War,* by Parallel Press.

Manufactured in the United States of America

ORCHISES PRESS
P. O. Box 320533
Alexandria
Virginia
22320

G 6 E 4 C 2 A

for Tamara, Dante and Carina

THE BATTLEFIELD PHOTOGRAPHER

TABLE OF CONTENTS

THE BATTLEFIELD MUSEUM GUIDE SPEAKS

1.

Here they come
in minivans, SUV's, Honda Accords
converging on this town from north and south.

Just like those thirsty, dust-choked troops,
marching, staggering... booted, barefoot... sunstroked
...on the Carlisle Pike, the Taneytown Road... jammed
with caissons, cavalry, ambulances, beeves on the hoof.

Banners snapped in the wind. Riders pulled up shouting,
pointing. Drovers cursed and cracked their blacksnakes,
the wagons heaped with ammunition, rations, dog tents,
stoves, kettles, pans, entrenching tools, and with stacks
and stacks and not nearly enough pine boxes.

Before the lines could even form
surgeons rushed setting up tables.

2.

What myth
what delusion
draws them to Little Roundtop
Devil's Den, Cemetery Ridge?

What do they imagine happened here?
("Now I see" Whitman wrote, "war is just butchery!
The glistening weapons—tools for slaughter!")

Don't they know that?

Or is there still a truth that draws?

3.

See the Rotarian in baseball cap and oldguy shorts,
how his shoulders hunch around the place in his chest,
scarred still, aching still since the morning his daughter,
just nine, was diagnosed. How he cared for her
giving every pill in proper order at 2 AM... at 5 AM...
petting her hair, touching a small sponge to her cracked lips.

Intently he aims his camera at the spot
Chamberlain and remnants of the 20th Maine
—bleeding, outnumbered, out of ammunition—
refused to give up. Facing odds as impossible
as surviving leukemia in 1960. As impossible
as surviving the death of one's child. He snaps
a picture of where they fixed bayonettes
and charged—by God!—charged!

4.

So they come, bumper to bumper.
The young for what they suspect.
The old for what they know.

5.

And you, reader?
Haven't you been marched
toward what you could not bear?

Didn't you fear

you might run?
Did you run?

Haven't you carried
a comrade hanging on your neck?

Does the cold ache your scars?

You know, then, don't you
what hallows this ground?

And why they come.

6.

I have arranged the exhibits.
Polished the glass.

I unlock the doors,
and open them wide.

For you?

FIRST DAYS

1.

Lemonade and bunting,
a fife and drum corps,
pretty girls at the podium
rousing the boys!
Kissing the flushed lads
signing the roster:
Three cheers for each
and a Yankee Doodle!

Round bonfires at dark
town fathers pass flasks
and handfuls of stogies.
You are soldiers now lads!

Arms across shoulders
the elders toast
On to Richmond!

Fists in the air
the boys respond
Richmond! To Richmond!

Oh luminous faces!
Mouths agape
laughing, cheering,
ghastly bright.

2.

At the depot hankies flutter,
roses arc into the ranks.
All the lads doff their caps!

Hissing and banging
in chuffs of steam
the cars pull out
throb down the tracks
and are utterly gone!

In the stunning quiet
the ladies begin to weep.

Blossoms and petals litter the ground

3.

...like the parasols of silk
and opera glasses trampled

by picnickers fleeing cloudbursts
of shrapnel. Those right under
fall in bunches. Some do not get up.

Caisson wheels slice
an empty calico blanket.

A hamper, tumbling,
disgorges roasted chicken
biscuits and folded white napkins
unfolding.

In a dash for the bridge
couples lose mates
reach back, lock fingers
and snap apart again.

At the arch they jam and back up.
Congressmen, judges, town fathers
their wives and children
a swarm
of dishevelment and wild eyes!

Fretting and moaning
—*What hell is this!*
the ladies turn away
from a headless body
swaying in an eddy.

To cross! To cross back!

With the flats of swords
Captains and file closers
curse and swat them!
Clearing a line of retreat

for the boys
stumbling, hopping....

Some held at head and feet
slack between comrades
their hands pressing dark stains
or trailing limp along the ground.

And that was First Bull Run.

All desperate!

Desperate to cross back!

MARY CHESNUT AT MULBERRY HOUSE

I don't know when I have seen a woman without knitting in hand.
Socks for the soldiers is the cry.

Mary Chesnut, Diary, 27 August 1861

1.

Mary puts down her Emerson and takes up the socks,
her pair for the day. Birdlike hands flutter in her lap.
Needles twinkle in the slant of sun lengthening
across the silk carpet... climbing the paneled wall....

In the fields around the mansion, a thousand slaves
hoe, boil soap, milk cows, haul feed in the July sun.

As if they had not heard with their own ears
the rockets and shells bombard Sumter in the harbor.
As if they could not read Mars Chesnut's—the Colonel's—
looks from horseback: Do you understand at all?
—Inscrutable creatures!

How much do they understand?

2.

Under that July sun Eustice Hammy at Rich Mountain
stands in a skirmish line against McClellan's troops
in line of battle firing by file: line of puffs, line of puffs....
Just like drill! Eustice smiles in wonder
even as the "bees" buzz round his head.

He levels his musket, aims

A minie ball strikes his shinbone just above
the top of a sock knitted by Mary Chesnut
—the sound like a hurled rock
on a wood plank fence!
Two inches of tibia blow out the back
of his calf in a red spray, tossing
both legs in a jig that sends him sprawling.

Oh, destruction is the miracle
of creation turned on its head.

Not all the king's men
could put together again
those splinters of tibia and fibula,
the gastrocnemius in tatters.

Still in its boot, in its cotton sock,
the perfect architecture of the foot.
Phalanges and metatarsals,
lateral, medial and middle cuneforms,
so beautifully knitted drop
beside the surgeon's table.

3.

There!
The shape of the adult male foot
dangles from her needles. Done.
The sun touches the ceiling, almost.

Boom!
goes the gun of a battery drilling
and her start drives a needle's point

into Mary's palm. The cotton sock
wicks the red pearl, and another,
and still one more. She pulls angrily
at the stains and watches stitches skip
and pop undone until the sock
is a cotton tangle in her lap.

Mary wants with her nails
to shred the yarn's fibers,
return the fibers to balls, the balls
to the pods that vex the slaves
at harvest, picking even by moonlight,
singing so balefully as the mountain
rises... the immoveable mountain
of—Of this life! Of discussing Emerson!
Of wit! Manners, Parisian dresses, and ballrooms!
Of *savoir faire!*

She finds herself weeping
as if she could feel the cold fingertip
of that demon Sherman in the wilds
hunched over his table....

Certain
(though acclaim
has eluded him)
his day will come.

Trailing a fingertip
across the Mason Dixon.
Down to Georgia.
Slicing Atlanta.
To South Carolina.

—He stabs his finger
onto the map

Charlestown Harbor!

The "Millwoods."
The "Cool Springs."
The "Mulberry Houses."

The very heart.

WHAT THEY LEARNED AT SHILOH

1.

At Shiloh Satan sang oh
a taunting song.

They heard him,
the Christian Soldiers
who never flinched,
who stood tall in the hail
of shot and shell, Faith
a mantle over their hearts.

Show me The Lord's minion!
This fair-haired Captain?
Hat upon the point of sword,
the pride of all his men?

Watch
in one stroke
I shatter that temple
—there!—
Nail glassy slivers
through that clear blue eye.

See?
Blood and water, flesh
and nerve.
—And Jesus?

Listen…. The boy
cries out! Cries out!

And does Jesus come?
Not to him.
Nor to any heathen twisting in the dirt.

2.

Back and forth strode the Lieutenant
sword in hand, shoulders squared.
Soldiers spun and crumpled,
flew whole and in pieces into the air!

Steady, men!
he called to boys
pissing their pants
in a sunken road.
Fix bayonets!

All followed his sword.
The colors dropped.
He caught up the staff
and waved the silk,
snapping, bullet pocked.

... Come nightfall
please Mother!
...Oh, water!... Dear Jesus!
roll across the field,
drowned in a bass note
rising and falling and rising
like a single moaning creature
with ten thousand heads.

On a blanket alone
the Lieutenant bends over his journal.
In a small, cribbed hand

in the dark he writes for April 6:

All the battle fear did grip my heart.
Forgive me, oh Lord.

My trial by fire I have utterly failed.

3.

Camp near Pittsburg Landing,
Tennessee
11 April 1862

Dearest Jenny,

I am up to my neck in work. It is slaughter, slaughter.
I have grown quite callous to death, and now watch
even friends die with little feeling. When first I entered
service I recall the wounded of Bull Run lying
along the road, passing on wagons and litters—
how my heart did ache for them! Now I find myself
surrounded by the most grievous wounds
and can only command: "Gather the amputations
and arrange tables, here and here. —What! So many?
Then clear these stomach-shot, these lung-shot—
all the hopeless cases to some quiet place to die."

Well do I see what happens to my heart. At night
I open the gutta-percha case with Andrew's photograph
and Elisha's beside and gaze at those beloved two.
All these boys (I tell myself) are such sons
of parents somewhere far. Or fathers themselves,
or brothers. —But grief, when it does arise,

hesitates and shakes my hand. I am best to the hurt

surrendered to what I am become, impassive and cold.

The moon is nearly full. To me it looks
like some once-dear face I can no longer name.

A million stars. And every one
has turned its back
against this heart of mine.

Jenny, I do fear I am myself
my own most hopeless case.

TWELVE FACTS ABOUT THE SURGEONS: A PROSE POEM

They stuck instruments in double-buttoned coats soaked with blood and sweat. They cut limb after limb without cleaning forceps, saws. They clamped the scalpel between their teeth.

For the best outcome, not more than 24 hours must elapse from injury to amputation the manuals read. That clock ticked down as they arranged instruments in their filthy coats, held scalpels in their teeth. A good surgeon removed a limb and sutured the flap incision in twenty minutes.

To release the humours causing suppuration they packed lint into wounds, preventing the flesh from closing over.

To prevent bandages sticking to open wounds, they wetted them down, insuring infection.

When they ran out of silk thread they used the mane hair of horses, boiled for pliability. The boiled ligatures developed fewer infections. This oddity endlessly puzzled the surgeons.

Fumes of ether and chloroform slurred their speech. They staggered. At times entirely forgot what they were doing and walked off holding a severed limb. They were widely regarded as drunks. Some were drunks.

Their deadly pharmacology featured opium pills. These caused severe constipation for which they prescribed laxatives with a base of mercury. After the war addicts in kepis and forage caps, their brain tissue infiltrated with the heavy metal, squatted on street corners in Washington, New York, Baltimore, Richmond, with pinned up sleeves and pant legs, next to cups and scrawled signs:

gettiesburg

sailer's crick

the wilderniss

Wounds became maggoty. The surgeons cleaned them out. Maggoty wounds healed unusually well. The surgeons began putting maggots in.

They invented a new term demanded by advances in ballistic technology: the exit wound.

After battles the surgeons bent over tables twenty hours a spell. Their feet swelled with edema; they cut open their boots. They plied the saw with cramp-curled fingers. Unable to straighten, they scuffed off to collapse on cots.

In lulls they penned letters home lamenting the poverty of medical knowledge. Told of horrors on the field and in the wards. Confessed hearts gone numb.

Before mailing they read over the letters. And tore them slowly into pieces.

THE COWARDICE OF CORPORAL JOSEPH HUGHES

His jaw vanished entirely! The length of tongue
wormed out the bubbling hash of his throat
like maggots in the beef rations I boiled.

Soldiers vanished in ranks and returned to view
out of all order in bits raining down as I ran
from that speechless standing corpse, the detritus
on the field, past comrades hobbling, crawling, as if in extreme
forgetfulness of feet and limbs left behind. Officers
waved hangers, mouths open and voiceless like the dead.

All the way to the abandoned town I fled
and in the third house found suitable clothes
and left my uniform sprawled on the floor,
no one bleeding into the blue, and departed

a live man out of a dead
in some husband's homespun
heading north to catch up the evacuees, north
toward Providence, toward Hannah and my girls,

whose names I recited aloud as I joined
the exodus of mothers clutching babes, greybeards
staggering carts of heirlooms and chickens,

and so turned quite away from the field of honor,
of duty, of every impediment to the fealties
of my own hard-beating heart.

ARMORY SQUARE HOSPITAL, WASHINGTON, D. C.
January, 1863

In Ward E, cot nearest stove: Erastus Haskell,
Company K, 141st New York Volunteers.
Typhoid. Diarrhea.
(Killers deadlier than the minie ball,
the canister shot, the bayonet.)
For the typhoid, stimulants: whiskey,
and wine punch. For the diarrhea:
cotton felt bellyband. Though burning
with fever, he shakes with cold.
Still-tanned face waxy. Eyes glazed. Breathes
in gulps and gasps. Dreaming, he moans.
He will die tonight.

Next cot: Thomas Haley, Company M,
New York Cavalry, shot through lungs.
Whiskey stimulant. For lungs, turpentine.
Expected to die within a day, yet he lives.
Strong, 16 year old farm boy, he lives
another five days. Dies quietly,
in a manly way,
to make mother and father proud.

Next to Haley: Oscar Wilber, Company G,
154th New York, shot through right hip.
Wound probed to remove bone fragments
and foreign matter. Packed with lint, bandaged.
Stimulants administered. Opium for pain.
Back on a farm just outside Brooklyn
mother calls father from beyond the fields,
where he cuts wood. She waves a letter
over her head. "Oscar is in Virginia!

He is well! —Says he is gaining weight
while—oh, heavens!—he is gaining
while all the others lose!"
She shouts as father lifts his knees,
chuffing uphill through snow,
white puffs around his head.
"Been there 'most a week...
—must be two now—Place
by name 'a—Fredericksburg?"

See that man with the bushy grey beard?
Walking the aisles cot by cot—
who gives Samuel Frezer a small jar of jelly...
and Isaac Snyder cut plug for his pipe,
as per request... and an orange for Lewy Brown,
left arm cut off.... Moving slowly, smiling,
responding never to the gagging stench
of gangrene, the sight of oozing wounds,
("Mother," he writes home, "I see every day
such terrible terrible things. One day
I shall have bad dreams...")

—who comes to Oscar Wilber and leans close
whispering encouragement in his ear
like the father, pulling up the blanket
around his shoulders like the mother...

—who sits by Thomas Haley, 16,
and slowly reads Psalm 23:
"...yea, though I walk through the valley
of the shadow of death, I fear no evil..."
then kisses his hair, as he was kissed
to sleep in his bed at home...

—who comes at last to Erastus Haskell near the stove,
his breath a low rattle, and takes his hand...

sits there long at his side...then folds
the hands, closes the lids, and remains,
silent, through the night.

In his heart he hears every tongue that was tied:
Wilber, Haley, Frezer, Snyder, Brown, Haskell.
With original energy, each speaks to him his life
in this war, his death. Without check they speak.
At times he covers his face with his hands.

Come dawn, he hunches his shoulders,
pushes palms down on rests—
his elbows shake—

and he rises to go and tell it now,
rises to go and tell it all.

THE COURAGE OF SERGEANT KURT MILLER

The ball took me in the reer of my hip
as I turn'd to rally the companie, our Captain
on one knee coughing out blood, Lt. Hooker
tramped under a casson that run away.

So it come down to me.

Without command the boys were clos'd off,
too far forward to retreat and chew'd
by the volleys of Virginians before us.

I thought of mother and wisht I might live
just so long to be hit in the chest or face
and so not bring her shame, nor any folks at home.

My new boots nicely took up the blood
so leening upon my rifle I remained
to all apperance strong and able.
In this way I commanded the charge.

Splendidly bayonetes bristling, the boys
pitched in licketty cut and routed the rebs!
Then righting about on my command
enfiladed the ranks of sesech at our reer.

I keeled over then and was carried back
and borded upon this hospital ship
where I woke and found myself alive not dead.

But they whipped us bad in that terrible fight.
Chancelorsville. Damned if they didn't whip us again.

Theres worst damned things than dieing.

STONEWALL

He sliced open the dream lemon with the dream knife
and squeezed real juices into his parched mouth.
Attendants, seeing his smile, nodded all around.
In the yard, a detail dug the hole for his left arm.

"Julia! Where is my Julia?" he asked all at once.
"General," a doctor replied, "your wife has her, sir"

and shook a packet into a glass of water.

"Ah," the General said, "Good! Praise God for.... Praise God!....."
"Yes, General, yes. Just rest. Your new darling girl is well."

He stirred the anodyne.

*Now he ordered canister for the Napolean, double loaded
and swung it into the Mexicans charging!
He begged forgiveness of The Lord for the rush of glee
as arms and heads flew out of the smoke, and the pink mist,
atoms of blood, lifted and drifted across the heavens....*

*And turning in the wind, turning, into a boychild turned,
smiling, lovely, swaddled in white, his face turning
from pink to red to purple to blue....*

*"Breathe!"
the General shouted, and the doctor bent, turning the covers down
off his chest. Just as that other doctor had bent, and turned
covers up over his wife's pale face, and the newborn, so dark.*

*Stone, stone, he built a wall of stone
more potent than bullets that break merely bone*

and behind it he stood unafraid and alone, curious
at the fools who would duck and run, as if
—as if The Lord at His will could not come
and take back joy! And leave the heart numb.
In grief's wall of stones, a stoneheart, dumb.

"Tell A.P. Hill to prepare for action!
Pass his troops to the front!"
Stonewall called, lifting his head.

The doctor spooned the opiate past cracked lips.

As Hill's troops passed, among them
he saw his boy child in a glory!
Gripping an Enfield with glisteny bayonet.
And Julia in butternut, bright flag waving….

And there! his own father!
Why, look! There, brother!
Tramping gaily toward the roar of the guns!

But they—Hill's troops all—
mere babes! To the slaughter marching!

Right hand on the pummel,
Stonewall turned in his saddle.

"We shall cross over the river" he said
aloud, pointing with the arm upon which,
in the yard, the last shovelful fell,

"and rest in the shade of the trees."

from SOCIAL LIFE IN OLD VIRGINIA BEFORE THE WAR, BY THOMAS NELSON PAGE, WITH DRAWINGS BY THE MISSES COWLES (1892)

LIST OF ILLUSTRATIONS

THE HOSPITAL SHIPS

They might have freighted dry goods—
blouses and trousers, spools of bright
gingham—from ocean ports to upriver towns.
But these days they carry farm boys, mostly.
Like this load of New Yorkers in white
stacked hammocks stained red, none of whom
ever before traveled 20 miles from home.

Under a crescent moon the ships
churn into Baltimore harbor, slowly rocking,
creaking, so that many of the boys, dreamy
with anodynes, smile into their mothers' faces.

Some will be delivered dead. Others
missing the legs, hands, feet and arms dropped
beside the surgeons' tables for burial in pits.
Many expected to heal in days will die.

Soiled gauze must be removed, slough washed off,
fresh lint and bandage reapplied. The boys will need
someone to write a letter, read the Bible, someone
to return next day, and promise to come back again.

This time of night in Baltimore
whorehouses and bar rooms ring with revelry
(the good citizens tucked long since abed)
as these ships steam in from Chancellorsville.

At the end of Wharf 6, in the dark,
a sack of oranges at his feet,
Walt Whitman stands waiting.

I understand the large hearts of heroes,
The courage of present times and all times....
                                          Walt Whitman

THE MOMENT THE HEART BREAKS

Not the moment Captain Lloyd like an apparition
slowly crossed the parlor, past all others, fixed on Amy.
And she sinking upon her skirts, hands over her eyes,
sobbing *James James James James*

Not that hubub propping her, fanning her face,
extending glasses of water, whiskey, laudanum.
Wringing their hands and touching her
as if to conjure strength from thin air
and press it into her skin.

Weeping with her. Praying for her.
Not that moment.

Guests whisked home,
in her room alone. Hearing below
the clink and clack as servants set table.

A door opens. Softly closes.
A scratching of whispers.

Watching a fly *tick tick tick*

against a darkening pane

     her eyes unblinking

        tick tick tick tick tick tick tick

from THE BOY'S OWN BOOK, A COMPLETE
ENCYCLOPEDIA OF ALL THE DIVERSIONS—ATHLETIC, SCIENTIFIC
AND RECREATIVE—OF BOYHOOD AND YOUTH, BY WILLIAM
CLARKE, 1829

1.

We heartily trust that the perusal of these pages
will remind us of our happy holydays
and favorite schoolfellows;

—of feats of agility performed
at "Follow my Leader,"
and trophies borne off
in triumph at "Peg in the Ring"

—of those merry mornings,
when the first glance of sun

awakened us,
to snatch an additional
half-hour at the play-ground,

when, during "winter's surly reign,"
we joined the active few,
who, instead of moping in greatcoats,
or shivering round the fire,

sallied forth into the clear, cold,
invigorating air,

and marking out goals and bounds
in the crisp hoar frost that mantled the ground,
sought after and found warmth
in high spirits and in a game

of "Prisoner's Base"

—and came in with high spirits,
ruddy cheeks, perfect willingness,
and the best of appetites.

2.

It will carry us back in imagination
to the hills and downs where we flew
our kites, the loftiest soarers
for miles around of mishaps,
through breaking strings,
and long races of rivalry after vacation....

—to the garden walk, where our school-swing
was erected, between two gigantic
sister pear trees; —and in brief

to all those places where we played
with our favorite schoolfellows

who were the delight of our glad hearts.

LICE

1.

Ticks like plums a season
plumped empurpled. Spotting
(if not spotted) white drawers
with their bursting. Burn
out the head then and done.

Bushwhacker fleas
slipped back into thickets
of horse mane and mule hair,
thatched hides
of beeves on the hoof.

Lice, however!

Lice

never

quit.

For one cracked
two hatched.

2.

In camp, betting the quickest:
which of two dropped in the middle
of a pine stump reached the barkline first.

Betting the biggest. And story was
this Tennessee webfoot rode
his winner, saddled and bucking.

Betting, one drunken night
the prettiest. —This,
with aspersions cast
upon sweethearts and mothers,
resulted in an ugly melee.

3.

Like monkeys the men
casually groomed one another,
plucking mustaches
and burnsides while chatting.

Sometimes in rivers entirely naked
they seared their bodies with lye soap,
sudsing the bushes at armpit and crotch.

(Then on the banks the lice hid out
in hatbands trouser seams and limp socks.)

Other times singing out "Lice soup!"
they stirred their drawers in steamy pots.

(Then in haversack folds the toes of boots
in blanket weave lice stuck their nits.)

In hospitals nurses stripped the infested
and bonfired every crawling rag.
Scoured top to bottom red-pocked skins.

A while the men, licefree, smiled.

Then the nurses
twitched and jigged,
scritching here and scratching
lordamercy *there!*

4.

Longstreet listened to Lee
plan the placement of guns
back of Pickett to cover the charge.

Every proposal Longstreet gainsaid,
resisting the slaughter impending.

As he was about to object
"Sir, if the guns fail ..."
(as indeed the guns did fail)

a greyback caught his attention
crossing the bridge of the General's nose.

Lee penciled a map unperturbed.

Between fingernails of the free hand
the General Commanding (Longstreet gaping)
cracked the louse deftly.

Another crawled from the same wiry brow.

And behind, yet another
comrade decamped.

Longstreet felt his eyes well up.

He saluted and turned, clenching
teeth so as not to blurt out

The lice! The lice!

from THE MOTHER'S BOOK, BY MRS. CHILD, 1831

1.

Early does the infant heart
receive impressions:

kindness toward animals,
then, is of great importance.

I once saw a mother laugh very heartily
at the distressed face of a kitten,
which a child of two years old
was pulling backward by the tail.

At last, the kitten, in self-defense,
turned and scratched the boy. He screamed,
and his mother ran to him, kissed the wound,
and beat the poor kitten, saying all the time,
"Naughty kitten, to scratch John! I'll beat her
for scratching John! There, ugly puss!"

It is a common opinion that a spirit of revenge
is natural to children. But even allowing

that evil propensities are hereditary,
how are they excited
and called into action?

First, by the influences of the nursery.

2.

Therefore, here is a fresh reason
for being good ourselves: if we would have
our children good.

Do you regard it as too much trouble
thus to keep watch over yourself?

Every look, every movement, every expression,
does something toward forming the character
of the little heir to immortal life.

It is not possible to indulge anger,
hatred, or the spirit of revenge,
and conceal it entirely.

If not expressed in words, a child
feels the baneful influence
as the imperceptible atmosphere
he breathes into his lungs.

Evil
enters into his soul.

THE BATTLEFIELD PHOTOGRAPHER

Up from cellars the good citizens creep.
Crack doors and slowly nose out to peek.

Chickadees, the first birds back,
flit in and out the abatis of oaks.

In the fields Tim O'Sullivan prowls,
his camera like a weapon shouldered.

Subjects aplenty cover the ground:
Reclined in repose. On bellies flopped.

Twisted in gymnastic falls.
Fetally curled.

Leaned against stumps and wagon wheels.
Mowed in ranks like sheaves of wheat.

Bodies, no heads.
Legs, no bodies. Heads.

A solitary heap of insides here.
There a corpse with nary a scratch.

O'Sullivan unfolds his tripod
and pulls a stiff into better light—

Its eyes wide in utter surprise.
Mouth operatically holding a scream.

He closes the lids. Pushes
shut the mouth. Pushes again.

From the blouse he plucks a scrap
the dead man pinned going into the fray:

Corporal Joseph Hughes 2nd RI
tumbles into drifts of cartridge litter.

O'Sullivan drags over a nearby gun
and props a Bible in blueblack hands.

Ah.
There!

Sets a three second exposure then withdraws
the glass plate to make a collodian print

in his wagon filled with acids and washes,
a darkroom built to chase the show.

He bundles the prints to Mr. Brady
who shops them all about New York

editors clamoring o'er one another
for timely images of The War.

THE HERO OF GETTYSBURG

As the rebel troops descended upon Gettysburg, one of her eldest citizens, the seventy-five year old veteran of the War of 1812, John Burns, donned his old uniform, seized his trusty musket and rushed to the thickest of the battle, where he fought with honor and courage unsurpassed upon the field, until at last receiving wounds that ended his heroic fight.

Harpers Weekly, 23 August 1863

1.

The damn tallow-faced sissy!

You have musket and powder, says he, but no balls.
—I run bullets all night, pourin pewter till dawn.
What? says I. You chicken-liver!
I've balls aplenty! Let's march!
And him grinnin that tallow face.

So I hied out for the ridge alone.
Headin for an infernal cracklement of guns.
"Welcome, Father Time!," says a Wisconsin johnny,
"Fall in at my elbow and anchor the line,
for you'll not skedadle on them hobbled shanks!"
—What? says I. And jumps both feet offn the ground!
I hoist my rifle over head, jumpin up and down.
But before I can make him eat his words
woof! off he goes like a torpedo hisself
aspatterin me all with brains and whatnot.

I commence to firin the Springfield
and soon use up all twenty five loads.
Then a dead boy's box. And then another.

I turn to fall back in the gen'ral retreat and—
swat! A ball takes me in the arm!
Then *bang! bang!* —Two more
in leg and back.

What? says I, upon the ground.
The rebs will hang me for a bushwacker sure.
From yon thickest limb o' this tree where I bleed.
So I heaves the gun, tho it was a crate-new piece
I'd already come to count as my own.
And quick scrabble a hole
buryin my cartridge box.

Over the spot I lay.

At times from pain I faint dead out.
Then harken the lines tuggin to and fro.
Shell bits arainin down. Cavalry quakin the earth.
Now our boys, now rebels atrottin past.

A boottoe digs my ribs. "Hey ol' man"
says a rebel sergeant. "What you doin here?
You in this fight?" "Captain" says I
"mercy no. My wife is sick to dyin.
I come to fetch Doc Leeds on the ridge."
"Thasso?" says the sergeant, "Well shit
if you didn't go and pick the worst damn route."
And he looks up at the sky to think.
"Le's stick the bushwhack 'n be shut 'a him"
says the sergeant's mate, a scraggy reb.
And draws back his Enfield, the bayonette
like thread slicked for a needle's eye.
"Naw, hail..." says the sergeant raising a hand,
"Leave the ol' sumbitch croak. "

What? says I,
Croak is it?
Well, I may be sixty-nine years old
but 'fore I croak sure you'll roast in hell!

And offn that field I crawl,
hand o'er hand, trailin blood.

2.

I ran from him just as far as I could run.

Clear cross country to the other sea.
But still in dark of night
if the cat jumps *thump* off a sill,
or a draft blows cold on my face,
I bolt up in bed
all prickly, puffing.
Then I scurry to my baby's crib
to make certain she is sleeping there...
safe, yes, and well....
A babe myself I came to them.

Even then he poked my chest,
squeezed my skinny legs.
Like Gretel's witch pinching the bone.

As I filled out he eyed me like that tree
flowering by our house in nobody's lot.
Not wanting to eat the apples green
but not losing them neither to some quicker raid.

(Oh he always grubbed his fill.)

So that market day I was not surprised

as I bent smoothing sheets and quilt
he pushed me hard down on their bed.
Hoisted my skirts and I buried my face
not wanting him to hear me cry.
I never gave him that.

Soon as done without one word
he buttoned up and walked to town.
Hefting cabbages and melons.
Haggling the odd cent out.

In his Constable's report next year
in with the mad dog he had to shoot
(though in truth he fired twice and missed
and the lad next door—that tallow face?—
marched out and clubbed the foaming runt)
and the boast that Gettysburg was free
of gambling and illegal drink

"A bastard," he wrote, "in the township was born
to one Martha Gilbert." That would be
to his adopted daughter Martha.

Me.

3.

Well, he was a nice enough old man. Oh eccentric a bit.

No sense of humor a-tall! Jokes mystified John Burns.
If you tried a joke, why, he peered at you
tilting his head this way and that like a spaniel!
When at last he made it out to be a joke
he shook his head and shuffled off,
muttering under his breath.

So of course the lads pricked him all the time!
Hauled his furniture out to the square.
Greased his hogs at killing time. Such pranks as that.
I don't believe I ever heard him laugh.
I never saw him so much as smile.

But on Seminary Ridge was he not just grand!
Everyone certain he would run.
And that old man in patriot dress
five times wounded ball and shell
shooting his musket of 1812!

"The only man who didn't back down!"

My, how the papers did sing his praise!

Why, Old Abe himself
requested the honor of meeting
our "Hero of Gettysburg."

Look here in this gutta percha case—
my John Burns photograph!
Lean closer. Can you see?

I believe that I may have it colored.

4.

Are you mad? I told him, You old fool!

Hell's own furies are upon us.
Go out there and you'll get shot!

All the more that mulehead fixed to go.

Next day comes a lad:
Your husband says come fetch him.
He's dying at the Riggs' house
upon the cellar door.

When did he ever heed my words?
Did I not tell him *Go out there and you'll get kilt!*

So I sent the boy away:
Tell him no I will not come!
Where John Burns lays there let him die.

….But then at last I yielded yet again.

For sorely wounded and near death he surely was.

5.

Yes, I'm the vandal

smashed that scheming bastard's grave.
And when they cut another stone,
why, I'll smash it and every other one
gullible fools might ever raise.

I'll give you a hero of this town
my own brave sister Jenny Wade.
And with scurrilous rumor that vile man
did besmirch her honor and her name!
That she in truth did bake no bread at all!
That she consorted with the rebel troops!

Lying for fear her fame—
baking for our boys undaunted

as minie balls about her flew
—outshined his greedy pose.

My blood boils!

And baking she was killed, the angel dear!
Whilst Bur—Whilst that scoundrel
lived to peddle his tiny photographs—
jewel cartes de visite—25 cents for four
at Tyson Brothers Gallery—
for a dollar apiece!
I watched him hawk his wares
in President Lincoln's crowd.
Shaking the great man's hand
and conning a pension.

I wish I had no sense,
I'd've kilt that rascal there and done.

One night I'll dig him up
and fling his bones to the mad dogs.

There are heroes in this ground.

No More Forever

When I remember all the true-hearted, the light-hearted, the gay
and gallant boys who came laughing, singing, and dancing in my
way the three years now past, how I have looked into their brave
young eyes and helped them as I could in every way and then saw
them no more forever... my heart breaks.

Mary Chesnut, Diary, 26 July 1864

1.

Mary marches into the yard in the dark, leading Lawrence
and Molly. "Who remain, Lawrence? How many still loyal?"
In his slow and dignified way, Lawrence answers without pause,
"Mam, we all here. Din't nobody go over, mam."

Just as she expected. All remain. She wished to speak that fact
directly to Mrs. Stowe: Put that in your horrid book! All remain!

In the middle of a yard of slaves, Mary commands the field:
swinging a lantern, pointing left and right, directing
this one and that to hitch the wagon (no horses? find a mule!)
fill a dozen jugs with milk, hunt provisions (beg
from neighbors!) and smartly pack fried rabbit, chicken,
vegetables boiled, sacks of flour. Fruit! So scarce.
And so desired. Oranges $5 apiece!

Her silk dress trails a strip torn by some officer's spur.
Molly flits around her snatching at the hem, struggling
to pin her hair, fretting as Mary shoos her away,
and calmly surveys what she has collected.

So be it then.

In the rising sun,
Lawrence driving the mule, she hies for the wards.
One hand at her breast closes her shawl,
the other holds her bonnet down.

Oh that Stonewall lived to ravage The Beast!
Oh to kill them, kill them all!
Her heart flames with Mr. Palmer's sermon
Yes, enough! Enough meek Christianity!

To fight and die like Joshua!

2.

In the stagnant wards
Mary can almost hear the shriek
of shell and shot, the ramrods'
clatter, the ear-splitting volley.

The battlefield clings to these men,
an atmosphere enshrouding them.
They are wrapped in its sights and sounds
as they are wrapped in swads of cotton and gauze.

Sunken eyes catch hers.
Stop her in her tracks.

Does she know this boy of imploring eyes?
She stands looking long.

Yes.

This is James... this is Wade... Robert... Preston
...Eustace... Samuel.... Here are they all in this boy.

Behold, my Joshua.

3.

She receives the news from Dr. Gibbes
bursting into her parlor.
"Fire and the sword await us all
Atlanta is fallen to Sherman!"

Mary rises from her chair,
her back to the fair city
crumbling
to blackened
chimney stacks.

Ah, then,
that agony is over.

She drops her knitting. Lets
slip her shawl to the floor.

Like David, when the child
was dead, I will get up
from my knees.

Will wash my face
and comb my hair.

DAY OF JUBILO

1.

Thursdays was the whipping day.
They lined and caned us slaves
no matter we done wrong or not.
So come a Wednesday I felt blue.

On such a day misfortune fell.

In the shed, the monkeys picking our heads
that biggest called Caesar screams—
for he can find no boogies in my nap—
and thumps me with his fist. Damnation!

Mr. Jennings and even Aunt Mary laughed.
But the only one thing in my head was this:
Girl, be whipping you tomorrow anyhow.

So I grab Caesar both hands on his foot
swing him round and slam him on the wall!

He lays out cold. Everybody stares.
Jaws so dropped I might have hung oil lamps.

There.
Now whip me for the wrong I done.

Next day they brought two men
special for my whipping.
One with a great beard and long lash
looped in coils. Both wore guns.

They come in the gate and to my surprise
from round the dooryard comes Ma at a run
and lights on them a hawk on rats!

Grabbing the great beard in one hand
the long lash in the other. Kicking
and clawing like she was crazy
until Master Jennings screaming *Caroline!*
Damn you Caroline! pries her off.

I pounced the other, kicking him hard
in just that place to make him crumple up.
Cussing on his knees he pulled his gun.
Use your gun I yelled at him, *Use it*
and blow my brains out if you will!

2.

That night Ma touched my face.
She said Cornelia is the spit of her ma

and pushed a bundle in my hands.

You can't stay here no more.
Girl they will whip you dead.

She told me run wherever you can run.
Listen for the paddyrollers' dogs.
Look and pray for a Union camp.

If you're caught fight she said.

If you can't fight
kick. And if you can't kick bite.

We cried against each other a while
then she pushed me out into the night.

3.

Fifth or sixth night running in the dark
I come out deep woods at a river bend—
and across that river, why,
the hillside rose up all aglow!
Back of that, a higher slope alight with fires!
What a glory!

I prayed the Lord and walked in Jesus' name.
Minding not my fears, but trusting I would cross.

Halt! comes a shout. *Who goes there?*

Praise God it was a Yankee voice!

Who goes? —Who goes?
I thought on this every day I hid.
Who was I now? What was my name to be?
Daddy was called Johnson till we were sold.
Then he was Jennings, the new master's name.

In the dim I seen the soldier point his gun.
And another at his side leaned in looking hard.

Dripping I stood and called back in my loudest voice,
I am Cornelia Caroline from Eden Tennessee.

The soldier looking hard, I heard him say

That be a nigger?

Come forward! shouts the other with the gun.

Come forward and identify yourself!

RECONSTRUCTION

1.

Up the road comes this most ugly wagon.
Drug by a cow, a goat, and a dog.
In a tangle of ropes. Heaped too high.
Creaking forward step by step.

He wore a yellow ruffled bonnet.
Red coat, buttons gleaming—
British, from the Revolution.
Too tight for his ponderous belly.
(I gaped at this wonder
our boys all lean as rails.)

Despite the spectacles on his nose
he screwed up his face and squinted
at my window yet still couldn't see.

I remembered the Nippie musket
Strother left for my defense.
Taught me to cock, level and fire.
But my terror of guns froze me in place.

2.

ching ching ching
went his spurs, silver,
strapped to fine, laced shoes
as he approached my home.
A sword on his belt.
A brace of pistols.

He stopped, spat a brown arc, stretched,
and then relieved himself at my front door!
Standing in the sun this December morn,
steaming like a barnyard beast!

I went for the musket then as *bam bam bam*
he shook the door. From the far corner
I grabbed the old Nippie up and shaking
drew the hammer back. I checked the flint
and whirled round for the stairs *Boom!*
went the gun, blowing out the stained glass,
propelling me to the floor quite stunned.

My ears rang. Smoke hazed the room.

A while dumb I sat.
Then to the window crept.

There below stood the cow, the goat and the dog.

The wagon of hams, clothes, tied chickens, rugs.

And the bummer? Behind me slouched,
grinning, squinting, pistols at my head.

3.

There is much I cannot speak.

Not a man in Georgia, not the worst slave,
would abuse a lady so. Dishonor himself
with vulgar speech, rude behavior, and worse.

I did weep. Bitter tears
at Strother for abandoning me so.

Who could squash this sack of guts
like a fat toad under heel!
—Fighting where?
Defending whom?

I sank until I wished to die.

Then did I embrace Despair, my lover dark,
weeping against his breast.
I wept and clutched him close
and, oh, I let him ravish me!

And then, *mirabile dictu,*
a perfect calm
descended over me.

Living, dying, it was all one.
Kill him, whispered my lover in my ear.

Kill him. Or die.

4.

Room to room the bummer pushed me.
Gemstones! Silver! Gold!
Big eyes behind the lenses
like cloudy, melty ice.

Out to the garden. Kicking at the dirt.
Show me! Show me where! Twisting my arm,
hoisting me almost off my feet.
Where is it? Tell me now!

Then dragging me to the well, *Fetch it out!*
I'll kill you! Fetch it out!

My mind went blank.
Observing merely.
My body assumed command.

It struggled and fought till he laughed:
So! We've arrived at last! In the well it is!

He grinned, brown juice on his chin.
What cranny have you cut? Fetch it out!
Leaning over the wellcurb.

Squinting into the dark, face screwed up.
Somebody's spectacles blurring his sight.
Leaning over,
feeling down with both hands…
and further over the curb….

Ah.

I witnessed my arms wrap his shanks
and lift.
See?
said my body.

Like this! Hoisting him over that fulcrum
of a pot! —In a flash he went heels over head
elbows splayed to brake his slide.
One spur hooking the crankshaft rope.

He cursed and threatened,
sputtering the quid out his jowl.
I tugged that stuck foot.
He commenced to beg.

How he got a pistol, I don't know.

But a wild shot tore past my head.

Clickclick I heard as I snatched
the other handle from his belt.

He fired again,
and for all I know again—unflinching
I pressed the muzzle where a heart
should be and fired a single shot.

He plummeted.

Then did the water roil and churn,
heaving up the stones and back
in rings and coils, heaving
and rolling in and out of itself,
like a rage exhausted by degrees.

On the rim of the curb,
the ruffled bonnet.

I lifted it on the barrel tip
and into the black I let it fall,
yellow ties afluttering down.

5.

That winter,
I watched Sherman's boys pass in good order
with the Colt's upon my lap. Determined
to shoot the first to approach with a torch.
But they did not burn me. I don't know why.

One noisy night a party of slaves
awakened me, encamped across the road.

Three males pushed through the gate,
arms interwoven. Cigars blooming
and curlicuing in the dark.

One detached himself, reeling toward my door.
Great eyes rolling. Laughing and cursing. In one hand
a bottle swinging. The other gripped a Bowie knife.
Just below he stopped. Swaying. Peering up,
slack jawed. "Mars John, I'se heh fo' mah pay!"

I thumbed back the hammer on the Colt's.

But hooting and swearing they melted away.

Next morn, they gathered scant belongings—
a few pots and blanket rolls—and trundled North.
A gaggle of pickanninies trailing
in emancipation's wake.

I resisted a mad impulse to wave goodbye,
as if they were departing kin.

6.

In all, I lived well on hams and chickens
off the cart, winterlong that dismal year.

The dog I cut free, and he lit out at once.
The goat next day keeled over, dead as honor.
The cow —Alice—gives sweet milk still.

End of March they sent me Strother's sword,
bundled letters, and that portrait of myself
in cotillion dress, complete with shawl and fan.

I did read some letters one rainy afternoon,
and long I looked upon that ambrotype, but....
In all it was like being familiarly addressed
by someone who mistakes you for someone else,
whom you yourself do know, somewhat.

All is in the attic stored away.
Even the regimental battle flag, much torn.
What is it all but death and more death?

This second spring, the scent of life is in the air.
Even as I write...how sweet the Cherokee Rose!

Sharecroppers in my fields with my hired man.

Out back of the well, Alice pastures in abundant grass.

And on the table by my bed, my Colt's revolver.
In easy arm's reach. Five live rounds.

BAD DREAMS

1.

In his rocker at an open window,
a glass of lilacs on the sill,
Walt enjoys the April noon.

The wind is right
sweeping away the stink
of the fertilizer factory
and the slaughter house
across 328 Mickle Street.
Buffalo robe across his lap,
he sniffs the fresh, bright air....

And remembers walks
on days like this with Pete.
Meandering walks, miles
uphill and down.... To the river,
along the banks to the fruit market
in soldier-crowded city streets.
Choosing this orange, that peach,
and eating with juices dripping,
standing in the sun, grinning.

Speaking hardly a word.
But taking it all in—
the cavalryman's stamping mount,
the rolling fishcart heaped with ice,
its melty, sea-smelling drizzle,
the prostitute, drunken, draggling her shawl,
the lazy sky of bright, fat clouds.

Wiping chins on sleeves, again they stride
off together, over the awakening earth.

Come dark, oysters and beer
by the tavern's pot-belly stove
until morning almost! Then
a bit unsteady, arms across shoulders
supporting each other as in
the phrenologist's symbol:
Comrades Together Walking.

Sign of adhesive, manly love.

2.

Those blue shirts he sent
how long ago now?
Did Pete ever receive? No word.
Not one word! Not a single visit.

Walt feels his face flush,
a fist clench in his stomach.

"Mrs. D.!" he calls.

Too old for these fits!
What excess! Morbid excess!

He pushes the robe to the floor,
whisks off the grey slouch hat,
and rocks, rocks....
Until his breath is even, he rocks.

He opens his eyes
—and there stands the very man!

Palms down over the wood stove,
cap jaunty on his head,
the sideways impish grin!
Old Pete!
Wearing—indeed!—the blue overshirt!
With black kerchief at the neck,
just as Walt suggested!

Doyle!
Walt raises his arms
and Pete's shirt opens
—intestines tangle out!
His belly is split with a wound,
maggoty, putrid.... Walt gags—
starts—awakens—gags again....

The wind shifted!

Awake, yet
images keep flashing:
hospital ships disgorge bodies
like a half-chewed vomitus
all over the Baltimore docks.
Eyes...mouths...imploring...thousands!

"Water! Water!" they all cry.
Walt hasn't enough water.
He moves too slow —Why can't he move?
His legs stick in deep puddles
of clotted blood! He cannot step!
Oh he cannot move his legs at all!

"Here... here! Why don't you take the glass?"
asks Mrs. Davis, at his side. "Is it the blurs?
Oh, drink...be still now...." She fans his white head
with his hat. "Drink, please...." With a sigh

she takes and puts his flailing big hand on the glass.

"Yes, the blurs," Walt lies,
rubbing his eyes, "it's the blurs,"
slowly raising the glass to his lips.
She wrinkles her nose
and thumps the window shut.

3.

All his life he dreamed of The Friend.
The One Who Never Fails.
To whom nothing need be spoken.
Intimate as the Self.

But even surrounded as if in a dream
by hospitals full of camerados!—
not in one ward, in one row, in one cot,
did he find the unfailing friend. Not Pete.
Not Lew nor Harry nor Fred. Not one.

Walt draws up the robe, pulls on his hat,
and cocks it just right.

From the glass he plucks a sprig of lilac
and presses it to his lips,
purple flecks on his white beard.

Soon he is humming softly,
some song which only he hears.
Like some solitary bird.
Like the hermit thrush.

THE OLD SOLDIERS

1.

The old soldiers remembered mud.

They told grandchildren yarns
of a Private, Johnny Mudd.

Mud pulled on their aching legs, like a cruel prank.
Mud sucked shoes and boots right off their feet.
Mud mired wagons, cannon, caissons.
Mud swallowed mules, heaving and braying
until their flared nostrils closed over.
Until it looked like the drover was fishing
with rope for some mudfish he could not land.
Until he slashed the rope and glared, fists
on hips, at the last coil slipping
into the belching
goddam mud goddamit.

They did not remember battle, the old soldiers.
They remembered stories about battle.
Stories with beginnings, middles, endings,
they told and retold.
As if they understood what happened.

They remembered comrades most of all,
boys who'd played Ring Taw and Fives.
Fishing mates, pranksters, hunting pards.
Enlisting together, boarding trains together
to tent camps in Harrisburg... Providence...
Richmond... Charlotte.... Emerging
dressed up in kepis, frocks and sacks.
Bristling with Bowies, Colt's revolvers, bayonettes.

Swearing great oaths. Posing for ambrotypes.
Goosing one another with the muzzles of rifles.
Sharing canteens, blanketrolls, last hardtack crackers.
At Shiloh, Antietam, Fredericksburg, for love
of these comrades they laid down their lives.

To the old soldiers in rockers by the fire
a face did sometimes luminesce—
ghastly—eyes rolling—*Dear God!*
—*Oh Robert! Oh No!* —

And someone, niece or daughter, did ask
 "What's wrong?
Why do you stare at your hands so?"
And the old soldiers did not respond,

could not turn palms out and say
"See the blood!... I held his head...."

No. They let their hands drop,
and shook their heads. Hiding in the abatis
of old age, the old soldiers.

On Memorial Day in uniform again
or Sunday best up Main Street they marched.
Displaying medals. Using canes. Their step
stiff, strained. Old age muddying every road.

2.

3 July 1913
Cemetery Ridge

The old soldiers once boys here
reënacted Pickett's Charge

one final time.

They looked across at each other,
rheumy eyes squinting in the sun.

Long and long each looked
at the other line of old soldiers.

At the signal to fire...
nothing.

Silence.

No one moved.

Wind ruffled their battle flags,
fluttered the streamers.

They looked at each other.

Then someone dropped his rifle.
Then another and another.
Then all rifles together fell.

On stiff, faltering legs the blue and gray lines closed.
They embraced, the old soldiers, brothers hugging brothers.

This last time—they laughed and wept—
we damn well got it right this last chance time!

SHARPSBURG AT SUNRISE IN APRIL 1867

The morning blooms out of blackness
as out of nothingness itself.

Faint light

pours a shy green
into pokeweed and mullein,
into the tender, shooting
new grass covering all;

stirs clouds into
bluebrown Antietam Creek;

touches gold
a cord of braid
in the beak of a robin,
her breast reddening
like remembered joy.

On a sandy patch
she snapped the threads
from a rag of sleeve.

Small bones there
in perfect order lay,
like the exhibit
of a marvel:

The Human Hand

(that can set
a gunner's level
or trace at parting

the outline of a lover's chin).

With her prize the robin hops
to the dead mouth of a brass gun.

She glances quick left and right,
then drops straight in

out of sight.

A Historical Note

These are poems, not history, but I have grounded them all in historical fact and then, in many cases, taken liberties with them. I have, for instance, imaginatively entered Mary Chesnut's life and mind to expand on her journal entries. Some characters are completely invented, such as Sergeant Miller and Corporal Hughes, but they are composites of actual soldiers I came to know from their letters and journals.

These poems, then, tell the truth, but, as Emily Dickinson prescribed for poets, tell it slant.